CONTENTS:

GREYSTONE BOOKS

DOUGLAS & McINTYRE PUBLISHING GROUP

VANCOUVER/TORONTO/NEW YORK

UP CLOSE

TEETH
That STAB and GRIND

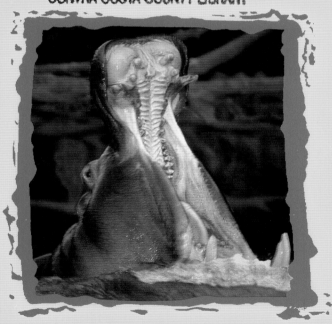

Diane Swanson

CRUNCH! It takes a solid set of chompers to attack a crisp carrot.

ALL KINDS OF TEETH

Imagine eating, talking, and smiling without your teeth. Life wouldn't be easy. Some animals, such as birds and turtles, don't need any teeth, but many others use them to get food and protect themselves.

Some animals even groom with their teeth. Horses nibble each other's necks to get rid of loose hair and pesky insects. Some kinds of bats clean and tidy their thick fur with their bottom teeth. And monkeylike animals called lemurs (LEE-mers) use six of their front teeth as a comb to remove tangles.

Rodents, such as beavers and porcupines, have four teeth built especially for gnawing. These ever-growing front teeth chew easily through wood, getting sharper as they're used. Beavers depend on them to cut down trees for

When they hatch, lizards use a special tooth in their top jaw to break out of the eggshell.

the dams and lodges they build. They also eat much of the bark, twigs, buds, and leaves of the trees they chop.

Porcupines spend a lot of their lives in trees. They use their hard-working front teeth to help them scrape bark and snip twigs, leaves, and fruit such as apples. The rest of the porcupines' teeth grind up their meals.

If a wooden shed or cabin is handy, a porcupine might gnaw that, too. It might also munch the handle of a wooden boat oar and get an extra treat: the salt from the sweat of a human hand.

When they're looking for water, rats might gnaw right through concrete pipes!

Mother cats use their teeth to pick up kittens by the loose skin on the backs of their necks.

Orange teeth are great—if you're a North American porcupine. The tough coating on its front teeth keeps them from cracking and chipping.

An orangutan mom uses her marvelous set of teeth to break down fruit before feeding it to her young.

CHOMPING TEETH

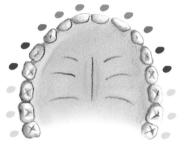

molars
premolars
canines
incisors

When it's time for lunch, you might be munching sandwiches, crunching crackers, or nibbling veggies. Whatever's on the menu, you have the teeth you need to chomp up your food: eight sharp incisors for biting, four pointy canines for ripping, and up to 20 flat premolars and molars for slicing, crushing, and chewing.

Like you, Asian apes called orangutans (a-RANG-a-tans) have 32 teeth to tackle their lunch, but their jaws are bigger and stronger than yours. So is their biting and crushing power! Orangutans spend their lives in rain forests where they feed mostly on fruit and nuts. Their large front teeth work like

The teeth of a little arctic fox can chomp up meat from whales washed ashore.

sharp-edged shovels. They break easily into fruit with tough rinds. And their thick back teeth are built to crack open nuts—even those with the hardest shells.

The mountain lion of North and South America has fewer teeth, but it has 12 incisors. And its canines are much longer than yours. All these sharp front teeth make wonderful weapons for hunting. They help the lion prey on big animals, such as moose, as well as small animals, such as beavers and porcupines.

One bite is usually all the mountain lion needs to bring down its prey. Then it rips into dinner, putting a set of special molars and premolars to work. With sharp cutting edges, these teeth make great meat slicers.

Most young spadefoot toads, or tadpoles, feed on plants, but some develop teeth that allow them to eat meat. Then they can grow much faster.

An African hyena works its top and bottom back teeth together like a big pair of scissors, chomping through tough animal hides.

For this mountain lion, teeth are more than tools for hunting. They're also eating utensils.

Snip and munch. A North American mule deer slices off a tasty treat, then its back teeth grind it up.

GRINDING TEETH

Pop a peanut into your mouth and you can grind it with your molars. They're strong, but they're no match for the teeth in a deer's mouth. It has a set of wide molars with curved ridges specially designed for cutting and grinding. These teeth can break down twigs, leaves, grass—even acorns. If a deer snips off something extra-thick, it chews side to side with its front molars. Then it shoves the food along to its back teeth and grinds it up.

A deer has no front top teeth, but it doesn't need any. It uses its strong tongue to press food against its lips and the roof of its mouth. Then it clips off the food with its sharp bottom teeth.

North America's giant bison use their long,

Eating bread wore down the molars of ancient Egyptians because it contained gritty sand.

thick tongues the same way to eat grass. Like deer, they have great grinding molars, and they chew their food twice. The first time, they just munch it up a bit and swallow, sending it to the first part of their big four-part stomachs. There the food softens while the animals eat more.

Hours later—when they're feeling safe and contented—both bison and deer bring the swallowed food back into their mouths. They chew this food, called their cud, a wad at a time, grinding it up well. When they swallow it again, the food passes on through all parts of their stomach. Chewing their meals twice makes it possible for bison and deer to live well on food that's tough to break down.

Prairie dogs grind up so much of their favorite grass that they make it hard for the grass to grow back.

A cockroach has no teeth in its head, but it has some in its stomach. They help grind up the food that it eats.

10

A big bison grinds grass—plenty of it.
This one is filling up bit by bit.

This wild Asian horse, called the Przewalski (Prez-VAHL-skee), uses its teeth to talk up a storm.

TALKING TEETH

Lose a tooth or two and you might have trouble talking. That's because teeth help shape the sounds you make. They help many animals the same way, but some creatures also talk by showing their teeth. A dog, for example, might expose its sharp front teeth to say, "Go away!"

Horses talk tough by flattening their ears, pulling up the corners of their lips, and opening their mouths to show off their big teeth. If they want to say "welcome" instead, they still display their teeth. But they don't draw up the corners of their lips to do it, and they hold their ears straight.

A young horse declares its respect for an older horse by dropping its head, opening its mouth, and snapping its front teeth lightly

Porcupines clack their teeth to warn other animals to stay away.

13

together. It might say, "I like you," by nibbling the older horse gently near the tail.

The hippopotamus of Africa yawns to talk with its teeth, but it's not saying, "I'm sleepy." Far from it! The hippo is making threats by displaying a powerhouse of weapons: strong, forward-leaning incisors and long, curved canines.

The rest of a hippo's teeth—a sturdy set of molars—are harder to see. They're often partly hidden by the animal's fleshy lips, and they're used mostly in feeding. As daylight fades, the hippopotamus wades out of the water and grazes on grass—about 45 kilograms (100 pounds) each night!

By grinding its teeth, a bison can make squeaky noises to say it's angry.

A baboon shows its slashing canines to scare or threaten other animals.

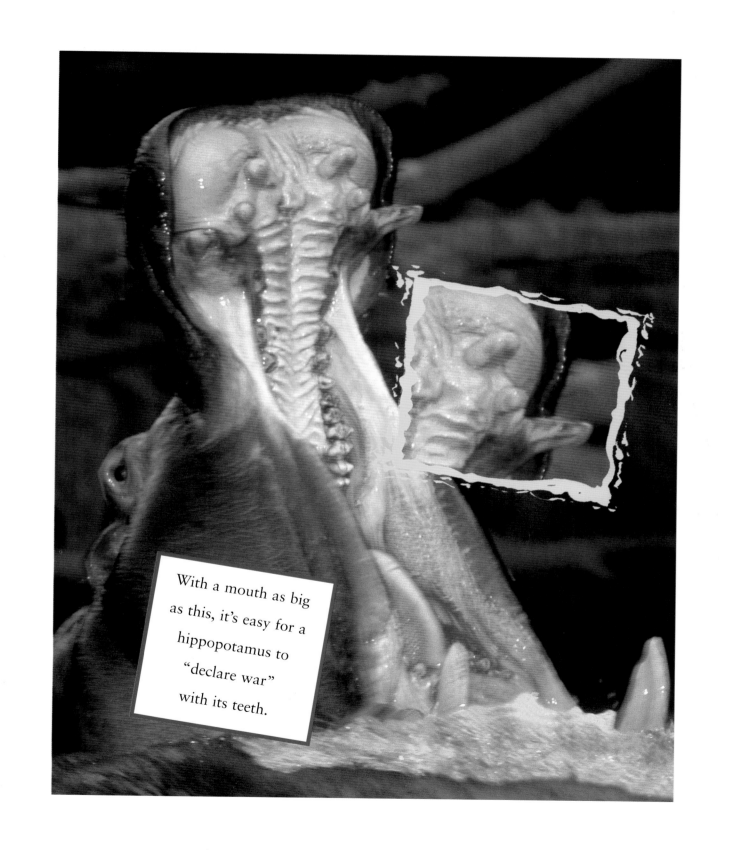

With a mouth as big as this, it's easy for a hippopotamus to "declare war" with its teeth.

A moray eel is ready to grab lunch, while the helpful little cleaner wrasse is getting rid of pests on the eel's skin.

GRABBING TEETH

If you think about it, there isn't much you swallow whole. You even chew food as soft and as small as peas. You're not alone. Many kinds of animals use their teeth to jump-start digestion by breaking up food with their mouths. Others use their teeth only to grab their food, then they swallow it in one piece.

Most moray eels have teeth like needles: skinny and sharp. They make great tools for grabbing small prey and holding it tight. Then the eels swallow it—dead or alive. These warm-water fish eat almost anything they can get down whole.

When moray eels swallow, some of their larger, hinged teeth swing out of the way. That helps the prey move along more easily. If the eels happen to grab something too big to

Little cookiecutter sharks grab onto whales with their lips and sharp teeth. Then they twist about to remove a circle of flesh or fat.

swallow in one piece, they twist it, breaking it into chunks.

Despite an alligator's huge mouthful of pointed teeth, it doesn't chew its food. It just clamps onto fish, turtles, otters, and anything else it can overpower. Prey rarely escapes its strong grip. Then the alligator tosses back its head and flips the food down its throat—whole. If the prey is really large, the alligator thrashes about to snap off a big piece. It might lose a few teeth in the process. But that's no problem. The alligator has backups ready to move into place. In fact, it has the ability to replace its worn teeth—especially the front ones—until it gets old.

Unlike some whales, killer whales have real teeth, but they're grabbers, not chewers.

Salamanders have teeth—both top and bottom—to grab food from the water.

Most of an American alligator's teeth are the same shape and size. The little teeth in this grabby mouth are replacing lost teeth.

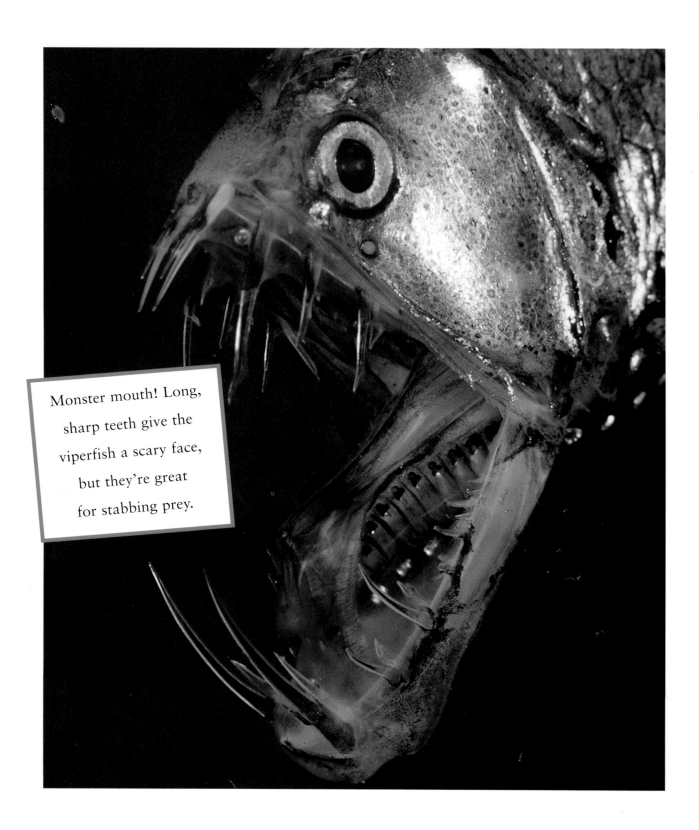

Monster mouth! Long, sharp teeth give the viperfish a scary face, but they're great for stabbing prey.

STABBING TEETH

If you've ever bobbed for floating apples, you'll know your canines don't make good daggers. Luckily, you don't need vampirelike teeth to get the food you need to live. But some animals do.

In deep ocean waters, the spooky-looking viperfish has teeth that pierce its prey, such as other kinds of fish. Sharp ridges near the tips of its top front teeth are made for stabbing. Two of its bottom front teeth are especially long—up to 25 centimeters (10 inches). Curved backward, they keep the wounded prey from slipping away and shove it to the back of the mouth. Teeth inside the fish's throat help push the food down to its stretchable stomach.

The viperfish attracts prey by lighting up.

Saber-toothed tigers of long ago were named for the huge canines they used to stab ancient mammoths.

It has hundreds of organs—even inside its mouth—that produce light in the dark sea. As prey swims close to the light, the viperfish stabs it.

The tiger snake of Australia not only stabs prey such as frogs but also poisons them. The snake makes and stores its own poison in its top jaw. When any prey comes near, the tiger snake spreads its neck to form a flat hood—and strikes! Poison flows from the jaw into two hollow front teeth, called fangs. They act like needles and inject the poison, which stops the prey from breathing. Luckily, the poison doesn't harm the tiger snake.

Fangs on a rattlesnake normally lie flat. When the snake strikes, they swing forward—fast.

The deep sea dragonfish attracts prey to a glowing flap on its chin, then stabs it with daggerlike teeth.

Tiger snakes aren't munchers. They pierce and poison their prey, then swallow it whole.

With its tough tusks, a big African elephant can protect small calves from danger.

TRICKY TEETH

Suppose two of your front teeth grew so l-o-n-g they stuck right out of your mouth. And suppose those teeth were so strong you used them to dig dirt or lift stuff. Then you'd be the proud owner of a pair of tusks—just like elephants and walruses are.

The tusks of an elephant are two top incisors. Most African elephants have tusks, but in Asia, usually just male elephants do. Unlike your teeth, tusks can grow for a whole lifetime. Some big African elephants have tusks more than 3 meters (10 feet) long.

Tusks are great for doing all sorts of things. Besides giving an elephant's nose, or trunk, a place to rest, they are handy for fighting or scaring away enemies. They can also lift and move heavy logs, and poke around in soil to

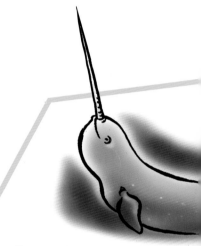

A long, coiled tooth sticks out through the top lip of a male narwhal (NAR-wahl). It might help him court a mate.

find water, plant roots, and salt. Just as you might use one hand more than the other, elephants often use one of their tusks more often. There are right-tusked and left-tusked elephants.

The top canines of ocean-going walruses—both male and female—form tusks. Pacific walruses can grow tusks about a meter (3 feet) long. They use these teeth to glide along the ocean floor and dig in the mud for shellfish, such as clams. Tusks are strong enough to help a walrus drag itself out of the water. And when it's necessary, a walrus can also use its tusks as weapons.

Wild pigs called warthogs (WART-hogs) can use their sharp tusks to guard their piglets from danger.

Woolly mammoths—ancient relatives of elephants—had tusks up to 5 meters (16 feet) long.

Tusks like these make good ice picks when a walrus needs to chip out a hole.

INDEX

Greystone Books
A division of Douglas & McIntyre Ltd.
2323 Quebec Street, Ste 201
Vancouver, British Columbia
V5T 4S7

Canadian Cataloguing in Publication Data

Swanson, Diane, 1944-
  Teeth that stab and grind

  (Up close)
  Includes index.
  ISBN 1-55054-768-2 (bound) – ISBN 1-55054-770-4 (pbk.)

  !. Teeth–Juvenile literature. I. Cowles, Rose, 1967- II. Title. iII.
Series: Up close (Vancouver, B.C.)
QL858.S92 2000   j573.3'56   C99-911197-3

Library of Congress Cataloguing information is available.

Packaged by House of Words for Greystone Books
Editing by Carolyn Bateman
Cover and interior design by Rose Cowles
Interior illustrations by Rose Cowles
Photo credits: Alice Thompson ii; Thomas Kitchin/First Light 3, 7, 19, 27; First Light 4;
Darwin Wiggett/First Light 8; Jim Brandenburg/First Light 11; Ron Watts/First Light 12;
R. Sanford/First Light 15; Kelvin Aitken/First Light 16, 23; P. A. Zahl/First Light 20;
G. Ellis/First Light 24

Front cover photograph by R. Sanford/First Light

Child models Anthony Fidler and Kimberley Cheung
through Coast Extra Events and Talent

Printed and bound in Hong Kong

The publisher gratefully acknowledges the support of the Canada Council for the Arts and
of the British Columbia Ministry of Tourism, Small Business and Culture. The publisher also
acknowledges the financial support of the Government of Canada through the Book
Publishing Industry Development Program.